TONY ROOK

ROMAN BATHS
IN BRITAIN

SHIRE ARCHAEOLOGY

Cover photographs
(Left) Welwyn Roman Baths, Hertfordshire, discovered and saved by the author.
The school party is about 9 metres under the centre of the A1(M) motorway.
(Top right) The natural thermal spring at Bath, sacred to the goddess Sulis and the
focus of a huge spa with two sets of hypocausted baths. (Photograph: Richard Abdy)
(Bottom right) Unusual *pilae* made of *imbrex* tiles in the western bathing suite at
Rockbourne Roman Villa, Hampshire.

British Library Cataloguing in Publication Data:
Rook, Tony.
Roman baths in Britain.
I. Title.
936.2.
ISBN 0-7478-0157-6.

Published in 2002 by
SHIRE PUBLICATIONS LTD
Cromwell House, Church Street, Princes Risborough,
Buckinghamshire HP27 9AA, UK.

Series Editor: James Dyer.

Number 69 in the Shire Archaeology series.

ISBN 0 7478 0157 6

First published 1992; reprinted 2002.

Printed in Great Britain by
CIT Printing Services Ltd, Press Buildings, Merlins Bridge,
Haverfordwest, Pembrokeshire SA61 1XF.

Contents

Acknowledgements

I should like to thank my wife, Merle, for transport and invaluable company while I was compiling this book (and at other times!), and to express my debt to many archaeologists, scholars and custodians (salt of the earth) for all kinds of assistance; also to those on whose original work some of the illustrations are based. The cover photograph of the spring at Bath is by Richard Abdy. I would like to acknowledge: English Heritage, figure 70; the London Borough of Bromley, figure 56; the Society of Antiquaries, figures 45, 52, 54, 61 and 65. I trust that my redrawing, interpreting, reinterpreting and even, perhaps, misinterpreting the careful work of others will not cause offence.

My thanks to those who replied to my request for up-to-date information for the second printing, and my gratitude to Dr L. Keppie for improving my Latin, and to G. K. Thomas for suggesting baths that I had missed.

The emergence of this book owes a great deal to the expertise of the patient and helpful staff of Shire Publications. Any mistakes which may have filtered through are entirely my responsibility.

Tony Rook

4

List of illustrations

1
Introduction

'For some reason the Romans neglected to overrun the country with fire and the sword, though they had both of these; in fact, after the Conquest they did not mingle with the Britons at all, but lived a semi-detached life in villas. They occupied their time ... in building Roman roads and having Roman baths; this was called the Roman Occupation...'

(Sellar and Yeatman)

Many a true word is spoken in jest. The writers of *1066 and All That* certainly had a point. Roman baths are to be found wherever Roman civilisation went, and the very nature of these establishments ensures that their remains survive in recognisable form. But there is more to the picture than that. The eminent archaeologist Sir Mortimer Wheeler wrote: 'It is an axiom of architectural history that the innumerable public baths of the Roman Empire made an outstanding contribution to the general development of plan and structure.'

This book is a guide to the visible remains of a typically Roman institution in the most northerly province of the Roman Empire. At the same time, however, it sets out to show the reader why a study of Roman baths is a rewarding one.

Not only were baths a focus of social, cultural, aesthetic and physical life in the Roman Empire; in constructing and operating them the Romans made use of almost every technology available at the time. To investigate baths in detail is to look at the manufacture, transport and use of a wide range of building materials from natural stones to concrete and glass, from lead pipes to bronze faucets, from painted plaster to splendid mosaics. It is to look at materials used in construction, at the provision of fuel for a sophisticated system of heating, and at the supply of water by hydraulic engineering which can be highly ingenious.

Roman baths evolved rapidly, particularly during the early principate, and evidence of many of the changes and experiments can be seen in the remains preserved on sites and in museums in Britain. This book gives a coherent and plausible history of the evolution, which, it is hoped, is both consistent and convincing, but, for a number of reasons, it is possible that it is incorrect in detail.

Where did the idea of the Roman baths come from? It is natural to look for their origins in Greece, but there is ample evidence that sweat baths have existed in many places between which there was no cultural or other link, as in Papua New Guinea, among the American Indians, the Mexicans, the Scythians, the Lapps and the Irish.

Most of the evidence available is archaeological, and often incorporated into surviving remains of buildings. Buildings are difficult to date, but their parts, especially where, as in baths, they are subject to frequent repair, alteration and improvement over a long period, are doubly difficult.

Evidence also comes from contemporary written sources, but even these are suspect. To take a very relevant example, Roman authors, according to modern translators at least, seem almost unanimous in telling us that the hypocausted bath was invented by C. Sergius Orata, an oyster breeder of Baiae. Since we know he flourished about 80 BC, we seem to have a useful definitive date for the invention of the hypocaust — or have we?

It is worth looking at this critically. *Traduttore traditore* — the translator is a traitor. What the Latin said was: Orata *inventerit balneae pensiles* — invented 'suspended baths'. Years ago this was translated literally, and illustrations showed Romans in baths hung between columns, like hammocks! Others translated it as 'vaulted baths' or even 'shower baths'. Nowadays it is accepted that his baths were suspended on *pilae* and that he invented the hypocaust. Again, this is not true. There is evidence that the hypocaust was known in Greece centuries before Orata. So was he the first to put baths of water on hypocausts? It is possible, although, as large boilers already existed, this would not be such an exciting invention after all.

One is reminded of Adam Thompson, a cotton broker of Cincinnati, who on 28th December 1842 created a storm of protest by threatening both the health and the morals of the North Americans by bathing himself in the first bathtub to be installed on that continent. His reputation and existence are still attested in journals and even textbooks — despite the fact that he was invented by a journalist, H. L. Mencken, who dreamed up the hoax for the *New York Evening Mail* in 1917 and spent the best years of his life trying to undo the damage. Imagine what might have happened if Adam Thompson had been a real person, and Mencken had been an authority of the status of Pliny, Cicero or Macrobius.

2
Architectural development

When the Romans invaded Britain, they brought with them the seductive trappings of civilisation; in AD 98 Tacitus wrote:

'To induce a people hitherto scattered, uncivilised and therefore prone to fight to grow pleasurably inured to peace and ease, Agricola gave private encouragement and official assistance to the building of temples, forums and houses ... so the Britons were gradually led to the amenities which make vice agreeable: colonnades, baths and banquets. They spoke of such novelties as "civilisation" when really they were only a feature of enslavement.'

Almost nothing that could be called architecture survives from the period before the invasion. Very rapidly, in the middle of the first century AD, masonry structures were introduced which were startlingly different from indigenous buildings at that time. Among these, still recognisable today and often better preserved than other buildings, were the baths.

The development of Roman baths started long before the occupation of Britain. Most of it is not documented, and we are left to create for ourselves a convincing narrative from the archaeological record. Where contemporary written technical information survives it must be treated with caution, since it has passed through at least three distorting processes. It has been recorded at a time when there was little understanding of what we nowadays think of as science by a writer who is unlikely to have had specialist technical knowledge. It has then survived through the ages, passing through the hands of a number of copyists who may have had little understanding of the text they were copying. Finally it has been translated by people who, like the original writer, were not technologists and whose experience and environment were far removed from his. They have often had to make intelligent guesses as to the meaning of technical terms.

Literary evidence supplies words; archaeology supplies objects. Connecting one with the other is often a matter of conjecture. In studying Roman buildings we find many objects for which we have no known Latin word, and *vice versa*.

Although this book is about baths in Britain, it begins with a hypothetical evolutionary history of Roman baths in general. This is necessary because the period when the legions came to Britain was one when the technology of the baths was undergoing rapid changes. Technical improvements were bringing about a revolution. Baths could be built

1. A strigil in use, depicted on a red-figure Greek vessel of the fifth century BC (left). Behind the youth is a perforated pottery shower. (Above) A decorated bronze strigil of Roman date.

which bore little relationship to those of the past: their architecture was revolutionary and their scale could be of an entirely different order of magnitude. They became a principal focus for Roman society.

The results of the revolution in the baths were to be felt in the evolution of public architecture of all kinds and at all later periods. It is important to see the baths in Britain in this context. They may be the poor relations of the great imperial baths which graced metropolitan Rome, but they represent one of the most important classes of building in the history of architecture.

Why sweat baths were used

At first bathing was a duty rather than a pleasure. People wanted to be clean. Soap, however, was not used for washing in the classical world. It was probably invented by the Germans, being first mentioned by Pliny in the first century AD. He gives a recipe for making it and recommends it as an ointment for treating scrofulous sores: 'soap is also good; an invention of the Gallic provinces for making the hair red, it is made from suet and ash in two kinds — the best from beech ash and goat suet ...' Martial, writing at about the same time, suggests that the reason the Romans did not use it for washing was its alleged effect on the colour of the hair. It was not used for this purpose until the later Empire.

To clean their bodies, therefore, as well as the more obvious use of water, either hot or cold, the people of ancient Greece and Rome made use of oil, often mixed with fuller's earth, pumice or the like. This was applied to the body and scraped off, and a special curved implement, the *strigil*, was developed for this purpose. Strigils are known from at least the sixth century BC (figure 1).

This cleaning process was much more efficient when the skin was perspiring, either as a result of exercise or because of the high temperature of the surroundings. In Greece small bathing establishments were a normal part of the *gymnasium* or *palaestra* (wrestling school), and after taking exercise the athletes made use of the strigil and then washed with water. There are sophisticated baths at Olympia dated to the fifth century BC with boilers to provide the hot water (figure 2). It seems strange that the bathtubs of the Greeks of classical times, unlike those of their early precursors the Minoans and Mycenaeans, were not intended for immersion of the body; the bather must have sat in the bath and had water poured over him or her (figure 3).

2. A suggested reconstruction of the Greek baths at Olympia in the fifth century BC. The walls have been cut away to show the water reservoir, the boiler over a furnace tunnel with a 'factory' chimney, and the sitz-baths. (After Kunze.)

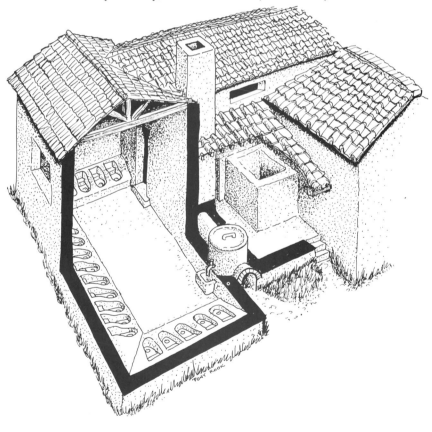

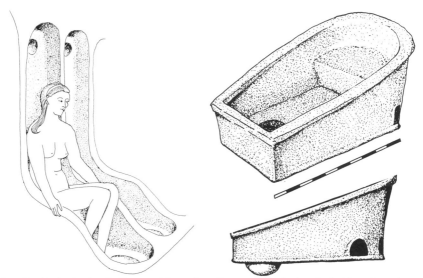

3. Greek sitz-baths: (left) carved in rock at Cyrene, Classical period; (above) earthen-ware, from Mycenae, Hellenistic period.

The use of a heated chamber was an obvious addition to, or substitute for, exercise to encourage sweating. It could have been heated like an oven, directly by a fire which was raked out before the bather entered, or by an internal brazier burning charcoal. These methods of heating would leave little archaeological evidence. Hot dry sweat rooms were called *laconica*, implying that they were a fashion adopted by the Spartans, from Laconia. Strigils are found in Etruscan tombs, and the existence of some form of Etruscan sweating chamber cannot be ruled out.

The hypocaust
The feature which is always thought of as characteristic of Roman baths is the use of 'suspended' floors under which passed the hot gases from a fire. It is tempting to see the development of this system as taking place in Greece, where primitive underfloor heating systems are recognised. The use of the word 'hypocaust', which means 'fire under-neath' in Greek, seems at first to support this idea. The word is, how-ever, a Roman invention, which does not occur until the first century AD, at which time it was fashionable to think of all the best things as having come from Greece.

The hypocaust could have developed from a heated chamber rather like a pottery kiln, where the hot gases from a furnace which was stoked from outside went under the floor and then through the room before passing out through a hole in the roof. Early sweating chambers were shaped like kilns; the circular cold rooms of the baths at Pompeii were originally used for this purpose.

Two descriptions by Vitruvius, an architect writing at about the beginning of the Christian era, seem to imply that a kiln-like method of operation still existed in his time. In his description of the construction of baths he writes:

'The sweating rooms must be adjacent to the warm room and their height to the bottom of the dome is equal to their width. Leave an opening in the top of the dome with a bronze disc hanging from it by chains. By raising and lowering this you can regulate the temperature of the sweating rooms. It seems that the chamber must be circular in order that the force of the fire and the hot gases may spread evenly around the circumference.'

Elsewhere, describing a kiln for making lampblack, he writes:

'A place like a sweating room is built, with fine marble smoothed and polished. In front of it is made a furnace, with vents into the sweating room.'

It has been suggested that this structure would not work because the bather would be suffocated. Use was made, however, of shallow tray-like braziers to heat living-rooms and bathrooms. There is one still in place which heated the warm room of the so-called men's section of the

4. Earthenware pipes used as flues. (Below) The common form of pipe, shown (right) diagrammatically, connecting to tunnel outlets at Herculaneum. Similar tunnels were used with other, later types of flue at Pompeii and Herculaneum.

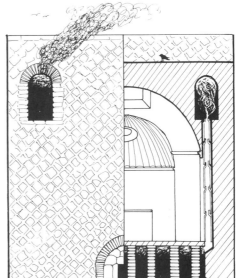

Forum Baths at Pompeii. Roman braziers were shallow, and their domestic heating furnaces never made use of a grate; the air passed over the fire, ensuring efficient combustion, producing carbon dioxide rather than carbon monoxide.

It would be more pleasant, however, if the hypocaust gases were vented to the outside without passing through the room. Chimneys would be needed to ensure that the air was drawn over the fire, and by the first century BC clay pipes set in the walls performed this function. They were similar to those used as rainwater downpipes, but set the other way up. They can be seen in the Central Baths at Herculaneum, where they opened at the top into a horizontal tunnel built into the thickness of the vault and vented to the outside through an opening in the face of the wall just like a window (figure 4).

By this time the Romans had developed what we would today call 'Turkish' baths. These usually included a suite of rooms, graded from an unheated chamber to a warm room and a hot steamy room. They were equipped with baths of water supported on hypocausts. As has been mentioned, this innovation was attributed by Roman authors to C. Sergius Orata, who flourished about 80 BC. According to Cassius Dio, the first public *laconicum* in Rome was the work of Agrippa in 33 BC and the first heated swimming-pool that of Maecenas in 8 BC.

How the baths were used

The way in which the baths were used, and the conditions maintained in them, were no doubt a matter of personal taste, affected by fashion

5. How simple domestic baths may have been used, based on the example at Welwyn, Hertfordshire. The bather undressed in the cold room (1) and was oiled in the warm room (2). After sweating had begun, he entered the hot room, where he was scraped clean with a strigil (3), before bathing in hot water (4). Returning to the cold room, he was cooled with cold water in a bath (5) before being dried and clothed (6).

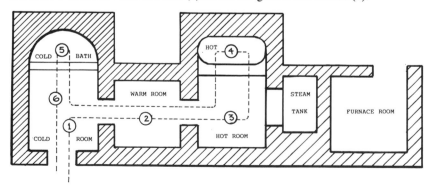

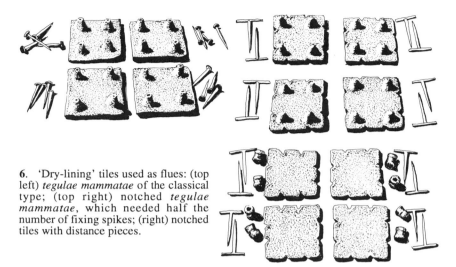

6. 'Dry-lining' tiles used as flues: (top left) *tegulae mammatae* of the classical type; (top right) notched *tegulae mammatae*, which needed half the number of fixing spikes; (right) notched tiles with distance pieces.

and perhaps medical advice; Celsus, for example, recommended regimens for bathers with sickness or infirmity. Other writers express their opinions, often their disapproval. Pliny deplores 'boiling baths by which doctors have persuaded us that food is cooked in our bodies so that everyone leaves them weaker for the treatment and the most submissive are carried out to be buried'.

In a simple domestic suite of baths the most probable order of use was to undress in the cold room, or perhaps the warm room, where oil would be applied to the body. After a prolonged period of sweating and scraping in the hot room, the bather would wash in a hot bath before returning to the cold room to be cooled with cold water (figure 5).

In some establishments, especially military and public baths, a dry hot chamber was included: 'If Laconian methods please you, you can content yourself with dry heat and then plunge into the natural stream...'

Roman engineering

The Romans had no discipline like modern science, nor did they have abstract concepts such as humidity or quantitative measurements for physical notions like temperature. When it came to building hypocausts, it is clear from many surviving remains that they produced a structure which they then modified until it worked, for example making furnaces larger or smaller, or adding or blocking flues.

Then, as today, there were two main causes of dampness of walls: capillary moisture seeping up through the porous building materials, and condensation occurring when warmer humid air comes into contact with colder surfaces. Even today many people would find it difficult to distinguish between the two. While there are different ways of curing each, there is one treatment which can cure both: the provision of a suitable cavity between the wall proper and the room, for example by what is called nowadays 'dry-lining'.

Towards the end of the first century BC a method of dry-lining was introduced. It made use of tiles called *tegulae mammatae*. *Tegula* is a tile; *mammata* means 'with nipples'. These tiles had four perforated conical lugs on one side close to their corners (figure 6). The wall was lined with them by nailing them to the surface through the lugs, which provided a cavity. They were then plastered over. This method of curing rising damp was described by Vitruvius.

Damp walls, whatever the cause, would be a common problem in steam baths, and it seems likely that the use of *tegulae mammatae* would have been tried as a cure. It would be a very obvious step for the cavity under the floor to be connected to the cavity behind the tiles. The walls became, in effect, one great chimney, with the rising hot gases jacketing the room.

The walls become heaters

More important still, the walls became heating elements. Their area exceeded that of the floor and, because the tiles and plaster between the hot gases and the room were much thinner than the heavy concrete of the floor, heat was transferred inwards much more easily. The efficiency of the heating system was increased enormously.

The new cavity walls had another surprising result which the Romans must have appreciated without understanding it. Because the walls were heated, the rooms had the same effect at a lower temperature.

7. Hooked tiles (*tegulae hamatae*). The longer variety resembles half a box-flue, and it is suggested that it may have been intermediate in the development of the *tubulus*.

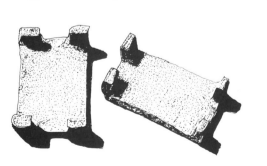

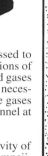

WALL

8. (Above) *Tubuli* or box-flue tiles, combed or impressed to 'key' to mortar or plaster. There were numerous variations of size and form. The perforation of the side walls enabled gases to flow sideways between flues, as would have been necessary over doors and other openings. It also allowed the gases to enter *tubuli* laid horizontally to form a collecting channel at the top of a wall.

8a. (Right) Shallow *tubuli* used to close the end of a cavity of *tegulae mammatae* in the House of Julia Felix at Pompeii. Early *tubuli* were not 'keyed' and were nailed to the wall.

The reason for this is that the human body is very sensitive to radiant heat. This is why we can be immediately made to feel comfortable by switching on an electric fire, which has little or no effect on the temperature of the air. For the same reason we may suddenly feel cold when a cloud goes over the sun; the air temperature has not changed, but the heat radiated by the sun has been cut off.

Several different types of tiles for producing cavity walls were tried out; some of them are to be seen in Britain, which became a province of the Empire in the first century AD, when this development was taking place. They included tiles with solid lugs, the nails passing through notches between the tiles, halving the number needed, and separate perforated earthenware cylinders which acted as distance pieces (figure 6c). Other types of tile were produced with parts of their margins bent to provide distance pieces. Sometimes called 'hooked tiles', they also were probably used for cavity walls (figure 7). The name may have caused some confusion, since 'hooked' is *hamata*; some copyists wrote this, rather than *mammata,* in Vitruvius' text.

The box-flue tile

There was one main problem with the use of tiles for lining the walls. They required fixing, usually with nails which had to be driven into the masonry. This was satisfactory in many parts of Italy, where the walls were built of volcanic tufa, which is similar in strength and texture to modern breeze-block. On at least one site in Britain, no longer visible, flint-rubble walls were lined with calcareous tufa ('cats' brains') to provide a soft background for the nails. Where soft building materials were not available, and with the increasing use of tile-faced concrete walls, which became the normal structures in Italy, a change had to be made.

It came quickly, and like many revolutionary changes it was simple. It was the *tubulus*, which is a simple earthenware pipe, rectangular in section, often called a 'box-flue tile' by British archaeologists. Possibly a large hooked tile which we call a 'half box' was intermediate in the development of the *tubulus* (figure 8).

Tubuli can stand against the wall without fixing. At Pompeii they seem to appear first to stop the ends of cavities formed by *tegulae mammatae* at door and window reveals (figure 8a). Their first use to line the entire wall is in the Central Baths, which were being built at the time of the eruption of Vesuvius in AD 79 on a site cleared after the earthquake of AD 62; at Herculaneum they were used in the Extramural Baths, completed just before the eruption — when the site was excavated a stack of them was found where the builder had left them.

Soon the idea occurred of 'keying' the faces of the *tubuli* by combing or impressing a pattern on the clay before firing, so that they could be stuck to the wall with mortar and readily plastered over. The patterns impressed by the use of rollers are the subject of modern study. Since each roller is unique, flue tiles carrying its impression can yield useful information concerning the Roman tile industry.

The architecture changes

The improved efficiency of the cavity-wall hypocaust, coupled with increased comfort at lower temperatures, produced great changes in the design of baths. They could be made larger, and they could be made with large windows.

In AD 63 the Roman writer Seneca visited the villa which had belonged to Scipio Africanus. Like many people do today, he was inclined to look back on the 'good old days' and to contrast them with the degenerate age in which he lived. What he wrote on that occasion is most informative:

'the bath is narrow and dark in the old-fashioned manner, for our forefathers equated heat with obscurity ... In this tiny corner he bathed a body weary with work in the field. But who nowadays could bear to bathe in this fashion? ... In this bath of Scipio's there are tiny slits — you can scarcely call them windows — cut through the stone wall so as to let in the light without weakening the fortifications. Nowadays, however, people regard baths as being only fit for moths if they have not been arranged so that they admit the sun through the widest of windows all day, and if men cannot get a sun tan and bathe at the same time, and look out

from their tubs over the land and sea.'
Large windows replaced narrow slits, but these large windows lacked glass. Roman window glass was translucent. One could not get a sun tan through it, nor see the view outside (figures 9 and 10).

Seneca also wrote:

> 'We know that certain devices have come to light in our own times, such as ... suspended baths with pipes set into their walls for the purpose of diffusing the heat and maintaining an even temperature from top to bottom ... All these kinds of things have been invented by the lowest slaves.'

In the first century AD the most rapid and important changes took place in the technology of baths. The use of heated walls made the 'narrow dark baths built in the old-fashioned manner' obsolete. Because of the increased efficiency it was no longer necessary to make them narrow — it seemed that the new improved hypocaust could heat almost any space. The bathrooms no longer needed to be shut in and claustrophobic to save heat. In addition, the increase in radiant heat made it possible to operate at lower temperatures and with large windows. In the Mediterranean area baths were built with what amounted to sunbathing lounges, heated on one side by the hypocaust and on the other by the sun. In the northern provinces, however, where large windows were constructed, they were probably glazed.

9. (Left) The *tepidarium* of the Central Baths at Herculaneum. 'The bath is narrow and dark in the old-fashioned manner.'

10. (Right) The Forum Baths at Ostia: baths 'arranged so they will admit the light of the sun all day'.

Social bathing

Whereas in republican times it seems that social bathing was not morally acceptable, by AD 33 there were 170 public baths in Rome. At this time, however, men and women were kept apart even in the same establishment. This seems to have been the case at Pompeii, where the public baths each contain two separate suites.

Large public baths were built in the first century AD. They often showed clear symmetry, implying that it was possible for men and women to use different rooms. There was, however, no physical separation between the two halves, which shared areas on the axis, usually including a swimming-pool. Mixed bathing had become acceptable and continued at least until Hadrian legislated that the practice should cease. To what extent this rule was adhered to is not known. The injunction was repeated by Marcus Aurelius and Severus Alexander, which implies that it was ignored, to some extent at least.

Where it was impossible to separate the sexes inside the baths because of the design of the building and there was no alternative, the expedient was adopted of permitting them to use the establishment only at different times. At Vipasca, in Lusitania (Portugal), the regulations for the Hadrianic procurators of the pithead baths include the duty of heating the baths for women from the first to the end of the seventh hour, and for men from the eighth hour to the end of the second hour of the night. A similar separation by time must have been applied elsewhere.

The concrete revolution

Changes in the method of heating went hand in hand with another technological improvement that had begun somewhat earlier but which realised its true potential in the baths. It has been called the concrete revolution by modern archaeologists.

Before the appearance of Roman architecture most structures were of the post and lintel or column and architrave type, all straight lines. Vaults and arches had been used by the ancient Egyptians and the Greeks in substructures, out of sight. The Romans learnt from their Etruscan forebears to use these as visible architectural features.

But the Romans were practical, pragmatic people — engineers more than architects. Where the Greeks would have laboriously planed their stones to make them fit closely together, the Romans would cut blocks to less fine tolerances and put mortar between them to fill the gaps. Mortar is an artificial mud used by builders for its special spreading properties. It is made by mixing sand with slaked lime.

A true arch consists of a series of tapered blocks, called voussoirs, which fit together to form an arc of a circle — usually a full semicircle in Roman architecture. A vault is simply an arch extended along its

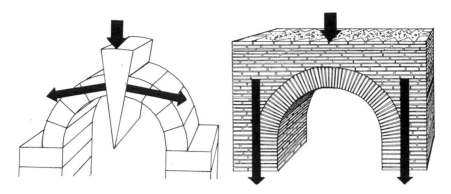

11. Forces acting in a true arch (left) and a concrete arch (right). The voussoirs of a true arch exert an outward thrust, as if they were wedges. A concrete arch transmits the load downwards without putting any part of the structure in tension. Although often clad with stone to give the appearance of an arch, Roman concrete was usually cast inside integral shuttering made of triangular pieces of earthenware tile, which, when exposed, resemble bricks. This sort of construction is often incorrectly referred to as 'brickwork'.

axis. An arch has certain advantages over a beam. When a beam is loaded, its top is compressed and its bottom stretched. Stone has very little strength in tension: a stone beam that is too long or too slender will crack. The voussoirs of an arch, however, fit together like wedges, and stone is very strong under compression. The disadvantage of the arch, however, is that the voussoirs act as wedges which push outwards and tend to split the building apart. An arch therefore needs abutments or buttresses to hold it together (figure 11).

Naturally the Romans built their arches with mortar between the blocks. In many parts of Italy, however, sand for making mortar was not easily available. What they had was volcanic ash from many extinct (and not so extinct) volcanoes. Slaked lime mixed with volcanic ash produces something very like Portland cement. It sets, even under water. It is called 'pozzolana', after Pozzuoli, north of Naples, where ash was quarried.

An arch built with cement becomes one solid monolithic mass, virtually a curved beam which has the advantages of both the arch and the beam. As with an arch, the stone is put into compression by a load. As with a beam, the thrust goes straight down, not outwards.

Volcanic ash is not readily available everywhere, but it was soon discovered that a 'pozzolanic set' could be obtained by mixing the lime with crushed tile, producing a pink concrete called *opus signinum*. However, even ordinary mortar has some strength in compression, which increases with age as the lime reacts with the carbon dioxide in the air.

Architecture and the baths

By the first century AD it was possible for the Romans to cover very large spaces with vaults, but large spaces are required only in public buildings. There were two main classes of large public buildings where they might have been used: temples and basilicas. For these, however, there was an accepted traditional form which natural conservatism wished to retain. A temple had always looked more or less like a copy of the Parthenon, with column and architrave construction. Basilicas were roofed with rafter and tiebeam trusses.

For the new baths which became possible as a result of the first-century advances in heating engineering there was no conventional structure. Almost all the development that took place in the use of concrete in architecture therefore took place in the baths. In metropolitan Rome baths built by the emperors, with free admission, became the people's palaces, providing a cultural focus where everyone could enjoy luxury on a regal scale every day. The *thermae* (hot baths) of Nero were erected on the Campus Martius, and *thermae* were built by Trajan, Titus, Antoninus (known as the Baths of Caracalla, they were started by Septimius Severus, inaugurated by Caracalla and completed by Severus Alexander), Diocletian and Constantine.

Baths as a social focus

Public baths were far more than just places to get clean. They were a social focus. Seneca gives us a vivid picture of public baths in his time:

'I'm in the midst of a roaring babel. My lodgings are over the baths! Imagine every possible outcry to shatter your eardrums. When the more athletic bathers swing their dumbells I can hear them grunt as they strain, or pretend to, and hissing and gasping as they expel their breath after holding it. There's a lazy chap happy with a cheap massage: I hear the smack of the hand on his shoulders, the sound varying with whether it strikes flat or cupped. If an umpire comes to keep score at the ball game, counting the tosses, it's all up with me!

Now add the argumentative noisy pickpocket caught in the act and the sound of the man who loves to hear the sound of his own voice in the bath. After that, the people who jump into the pool with an almighty splash, beside those with raucous voices. You have to imagine the dipilator giving his falsetto shriek to advertise his presence and never silent except when making somebody else scream by plucking hair from his armpits. There's the refreshment man with his wide range of cries, the sausage vendor, the confectioner, the men from the places of refreshment shouting their wares, each with his own vendor's cry.'

The imperial *thermae* were provided with works of art, rare imported stone, mosaics and an inexhaustible supply of water brought over great distances by aqueducts. They contained, as well as the baths proper, exercise yards, gardens and libraries. The most complete ruins visible today are the so-called Baths of Caracalla, which occupy 10.9 hectares (figure 12). Although they are outside the scope of this book, their importance in our study lies in the fact that baths came to be associated with civilisation and pleasure, something that was typically Roman; they were a facility to which everyone who thought of himself as Roman ought to have access. Like the modern *nouveau riche*, the rustic villa dweller wanted to have as much of the civilisation of the town as his situation permitted; he created *urbs in rure*. The degree of luxury provided in baths in the provinces is a measure of the Romanisation of their users.

12. A simplified plan of the Baths of Caracalla at Rome. Note the organised structure as well as the enormous size of these imperial *thermae*. L denotes libraries and lecture halls. The round 'sunbathing lounge' is orientated to the south-west to face the afternoon sun. This factor determined the orientation of the *thermae*.

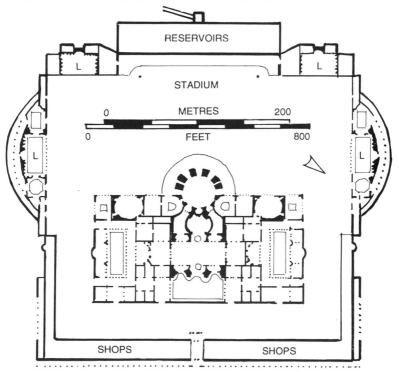

3
The structure of the baths

The naming of parts

An archaeologist working on a Roman building would like to allocate a function to each part and to use the correct Latin name to describe it. As Roman archaeology has evolved a more or less agreed vocabulary has been developed — even if it is not one which would have been used by a Roman.

As pointed out earlier, words have gone through a process of being written, copied and translated by people who were not necessarily experts. We do not know what word the Greeks used for the heating system using suspended floors and, although underfloor heating had been in use for generations before his time, when the word 'hypocaust' was first used by Vitruvius in the first century AD it is best translated 'furnace':

'Three bronze boilers are to be set over the hypocaust, one for hot, one for tepid and one for cold water ... The arrangement must allow the heat exchangers for the bath tubs to be heated by the same hypocaust.'

Its use in a poem by Statius written in the late first century implies *something* heating a room from below:

'... languidly creeps the warmth about the house, while a faint haze rolls up from the hypocaust beneath.'

Modern writers use the word 'hypocaust' to mean either the complete heating system or, more commonly, the structure underneath the suspended floor.

We tend to label the rooms of a Roman building with Latin names, forgetting that the Romans themselves would be unlikely to use words with accuracy and that both the function of any particular room and the name for it could have changed over the very long period of the Roman occupation. Different Roman writers recommend different regimens for bathing, and their language, like ours, was not static. For example, the living-room of the author's house has been called by successive tenants: the front room, the lounge, the drawing-room and the parlour! It is, however, part of a medieval hall; and the word 'hall' has greatly changed its significance in the past five hundred years.

Variations of plan

Although the great imperial *thermae* developed an organised and conventional plan, the plans of the lesser baths in the provinces are surprisingly varied and different. It is clear that they were mainly built without the benefit of any conventional arrangement, according to the taste, whim or ignorance of the owner. The variation is surprising, since the actual units of construction were standardised and must have been mass-produced in centralised works. It implies that after the intending builder purchased his materials he was without the benefit of architect or published plans. Only in larger suites where the military engineers were likely to have been involved — in larger towns and forts — does there seem to be similarity of plan.

Every establishment, such as one belonging to a rich villa or a fort, usually contained three principal chambers graduated in temperature from cold room (*frigidarium*) to warm room (*tepidarium*) to hot room (*caldarium*, sometimes *calidarium*) (figure 5). Since the Romans had no concept of measurement of temperature, we can only guess at the conditions which applied in the different rooms, with the aid of contemporary references and analogy from modern Turkish and sauna baths.

The cold room

The *frigidarium*, as its name implies, was unheated. In some establishments it probably served as a changing room, whereas in others there was a separate room (*apodyterium*) for undressing and dressing. The main use of the cold room was for cooling down. After a very hot bath the body experiences a physiological inertia. Dilation of the surface capillaries, which leads to lowered blood pressure, high colouring and deprivation of blood to essential organs, persists for some time after emerging from a very hot place, as does perspiration. In the cold room the bather can cool slowly, or, more commonly, can have a cold dip or cold shower. For this purpose a cold bath (*puteus* or *baptisterium*) was usually provided. Many reports refer to the cold bath as a 'plunge' bath regardless of its size. In many instances it was far too small to plunge into: typically 0.7 metre deep and 1.0 metre across. Apparently the bather has water poured over him, either standing, as in early Christian representations of baptism, or sitting on the step which is usually provided, as in Greek baths. The step in a bath is called *pulvinus* (a pillow) by some Roman writers. Some baths included a pool large enough for immersion and even swimming (*piscina*, *natatio* or *natatorium*).

The warm room

The *tepidarium* served as an intermediate acclimatising room before the bather entered the full heat of the next room. By modern analogy it was probably at, or just above, blood heat, about 40°C. Here the physiological inertia was overcome, vascular dilation and perspiration being initiated. It is likely that the bather was anointed with oil or other

13. Diagrammatic section across the stokehole and hot room of a small suite of Roman baths. In many domestic baths in Britain the hot bath is in an apse or *schola*, while over the furnace is a small tank of hot water which does not seem to have been a bath and lacks the *testudo*.

unguent in this room. Sometimes another room connected with the *tepidarium* is recognised as the *unctorium* or *elaeothesium* for the storage, and perhaps the administration, of the unguents.

The hot room

The *caldarium* (figure 13) was maintained at a high temperature. A modern Turkish bath could be at about 60°C. It is likely that in this room the floor was too hot to touch. When the slaves of Larcius Macedo tried to kill him, they threw him on to the floor of his *caldarium* to discover whether he was feigning death. It was usual for wooden-soled sandals (*soleae balneares*) to be worn to protect the feet. The walls were also hot. Fronto records:

'As my boys were carrying me as usual from the baths they bumped me a little carelessly against the scorching entrance to the baths. My knee is both grazed and burnt.'

The humidity was also kept high. In many small baths an additional concrete hot tank was built directly over the furnace to ensure this. No

Latin word seems to exist for it, and so here it is called a steam tank.

Provision was made for the bather to wash his face with cold or warm water from a basin (*labrum*) on a pedestal in the hot room. The *labrum* often stood in the centre of a semicircular apse or *schola*.

When the bather had been scraped clean with a strigil he would bathe in a hot bath (*alveus, piscina calida* or *solium*). In many establishments that was directly over the furnace, sometimes with a heat-exchanger (*testudo*, a 'tortoise') of bronze, often semi-cylindrical, connecting directly to it. The temperature of the water could be very hot. Seneca wrote:

> 'the temperature that men have recently made fashionable, [is] as great as a conflagration, to such an extent that a slave convicted for a criminal act should be bathed alive. It appears to me that today there is no difference between "the bath is hot" and "the bath is on fire"'.

To complete the process, the bather would return to the *frigidarium* and perhaps make use of the *puteus* or *piscina*.

Palaestra and basilica

Outside the baths there may have been some sort of exercise yard, a survival of the *palaestra* or *gymnasium* of the early establishments, where it took the form of a colonnaded courtyard, similar in form to a peristyle or the later cloister. In some baths a covered hall or *basilica* was provided. Two of the most impressive surviving pieces of Roman masonry in Britain are upstanding fragments of the walls between public baths and their basilicas, at Wroxeter and Leicester (see chapter 4).

The laconicum

An additional hot dry room sometimes formed part of the baths. It represents the original sweating chamber and is called a *laconicum*, a name given to it by the Romans because they believed it was originally used by the Spartans from Laconia. Sometimes it is called a *sudatorium*, but that could mean any sweat room, either dry or humid (Latin *sudo*, 'I sweat'). The temperature in this room was probably even higher than in the *caldarium*.

The furnace room

The furnace was an arched tunnel which passed underneath the wall from outside a heated room; usually there was no direct connection between the area in which the bathers were and that occupied by the stokers, who were usually, but not always, under cover in a room of their own, the *praefurnium*.

The fire burned directly on the floor of the tunnel, without any grate — more like a bonfire than a modern fireplace. It is surprising, perhaps, that Roman furnaces, even for industrial processes, operated in this way. There are advantages, however. One is that the fire, like a bonfire, will continue to burn unattended for long periods, as overnight. The baths must have been kept hot continuously. Another is that the operating temperature can be kept reasonably constant simply by adjusting the size and geometry of the fire. Air is drawn into the hypocaust over the top of the burning fuel at a rate which depends upon the difference in temperature between the gases at the bottom of the wall flues and that of the air outside. When the temperature under the floor rises, more air is drawn over the fire from outside, reducing the rate of heating. With a fire in a grate, however, as the temperature rose more air would be drawn *through* the fuel, increasing the temperature still further.

If high temperatures are needed for an industrial purpose, a blower, such as bellows, may be used to force air through the fuel; this principle is used in a blacksmith's forge.

In some baths, as at Chesters, excavators have noted covered channels under the stoking arch and beneath the sub-floor of the hypocaust. A number of theories have been put forward to explain these, including a suggestion that they were part of an ingenious system which provided preheated fresh air through vents into the heated rooms, that they were necessary for furnaces burning charcoal, or that they were drains. None of the hypotheses seems particularly satisfying. It may be that the builders were sufficiently convinced of the advantages to go to the considerable trouble of providing the channels without any physical evidence to justify this practice.

Fuel

The fuel used to heat hypocausted baths was normally wood, although charcoal could have been employed with advantage, since it requires less storage space and, if properly made, burns almost without smoke. The quantity burned is not known, although theoretical calculations have been made and experiments are in hand. The amount would have been considerable and must normally have come from coppice woodland, that is woodland which is cut on a regular cycle and allowed to spring up again rather than being clear-felled. To provide fuel this must have been an appreciable part of a Roman estate. Calculations based on possible operating conditions for the small baths at Welwyn, Hertfordshire, with rooms 2.4 metres square, have suggested the output of 23 hectares. Coal was used in Roman Britain and has been found in hypocausts, none of them heating baths.

Water supply

The imperial *thermae* required a continuous flow of thousands of gallons of water from aqueducts. With smaller baths less water was used and a continuous flow was often dispensed with; a small suite of villa baths could have been supplied by a slave with a bucket. Pumps were known, and a fine force pump from a well at Silchester, Hampshire, is displayed in Reading Museum (figure 14). The remains of a fine bronze force pump are exhibited in the Greek and Roman Life Room at the British Museum. Vitruvius describes the construction of such a pump, as well as other methods of raising water: the Archimedean screw, a 'drum' (a cylinder with radial internal segments which picks up water at the circumference and lets it out at the axle), the bucket wheel, and a bucket chain. Remains of aqueducts have been recognised in Britain, including what may be the foundations of a sophisticated arched structure to conduct water to Lincoln, over the stream called Roaring Meg.

14. Wooden double-acting force pump from Silchester, Hampshire, in Reading Museum: (left) as displayed; (above right) diagram to show the internal configuration; (below right) diagrammatic section to show how it worked. The cylinders are lined with lead.

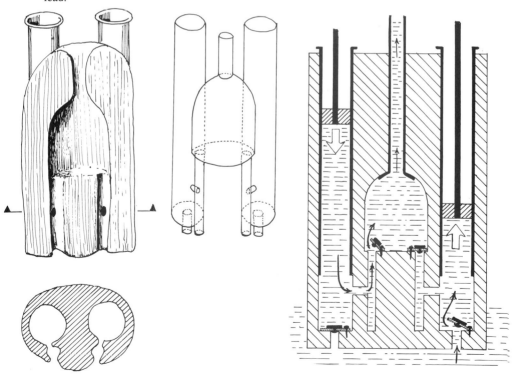

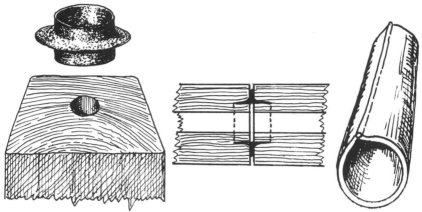

15. Water supply: (left) wooden pipe with iron 'collar' to form a joint (shown in cross-section, centre); (right) section of lead pipe. These pipes were made from sheet and not extruded. Earthenware pipes were also used (see figure 4).

16. (Below) Roman bronze tap (left) and section through it (right). (Bottom) 'Mixing taps' from the Villa Pisanella, Boscoreale, now in Naples Museum.

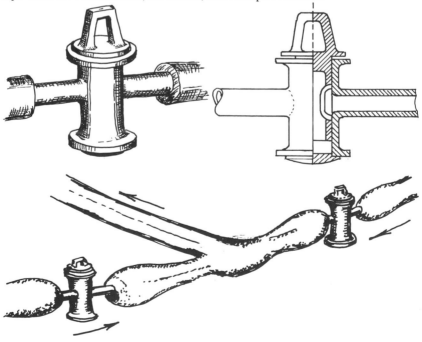

Water pipes were made of earthenware, wood (joined by iron 'collars') or lead (figure 15).

Hot water was supplied from one or more cylindrical boilers supported over the furnace, on short walls projecting into the *praefurnium*. The boilers were usually of bronze or lead, with bronze bottoms, and were encased in concrete. They looked like milestones and were called *milliaria* for this reason. The plumbing used lead pipes, made from rolled sheet, with wiped joints. Taps were made of cast bronze. In a surviving system from Boscoreale, preserved by the eruption of Vesuvius in AD 79, branched pipes with paired taps enabled hot and cold water to be mixed by the attendant in the stokehole to provide the correct temperature inside the baths (figures 16 and 17).

In some large baths, large iron beams have been found in the furnace. They have bifurcated ends, something like enormous tie-bars from cavity walls. Examples are displayed in the Jewry Wall Museum at Leicester, and at Chedworth, Gloucestershire. Their function is not clear, but it is likely that they supported the boiler or the *testudo* (figures 13 and 18).

The hypocaust

The stokehole and the spaces under the heated rooms were normally excavated to a depth of about 1 metre. They could be floored with tiles, concrete or flagstones but were often without flooring. The floors of the heated rooms were usually supported on short columns (*pilae*) about

17. The *praefurnium* at the Villa Pisanella. (Left) The boiler. Made of lead with a bronze bottom, it was originally cased in concrete to half its height. (Right) Detail of the plumbing. 'The water gurgles in a tangle of pipes that pierce the wall' (Sidonius). The unbranched pipe connects the header tank to the boiler; the taps in the branched pipes permit hot and cold water to be mixed (see figure 16, bottom).

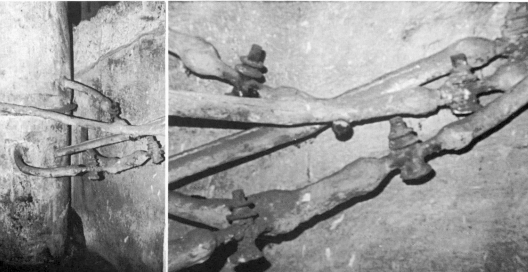

18. The hot baths in the women's *caldarium* of the Stabian Baths at Pompeii. On the right are the step (*pulvinus*) and the overflow pipe. In the centre is the arched opening into the *testudo*, which here runs diagonally to the left, as the furnace is skew to the bath.

1 metre tall. Commonly made of tiles 20 cm square (*bessales*), they could be made of tiles of other sizes or shapes, shaped stone or rubble masonry. Some earthenware columns, made like chimney-pots, are known, and *pilae* could be improvised, for example from *tubuli* or pairs of *imbrices* (the curved roofing tiles) filled with concrete. At Lullingstone, Kent, the *caldarium* was built like a tile kiln, the floor being supported on tile piers. This construction occurred elsewhere in Kent, at Little Chart (not visible today; figure 19).

On top of the *pilae* concrete floors were laid on 0.6 metre square tiles (*bipedales*), flagstones or the like. A surface of tiles or mosaic was often added.

Chimneys

The hot gases passed up the walls and vented to the outside at a high level. The common form of flue after about AD 100 was the *tubulus*, either lining the whole of the faces of the walls or set in vertical slots. In early baths use was made of *tegulae mammatae*, hooked tiles, tiles with distance pieces or clay pipes. In some places thin flagstones were used, as at Bearsden near Glasgow and Chesters, Northumberland, where

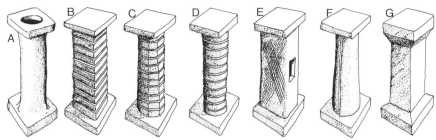

19. Various forms of *pilae*: (A) hollow earthenware; (B) made with 20 cm square tiles (*bessales*) set in mortar or clay — the common form in lowland Britain; (C) octagonal tiles; (D) round tiles; (E) made from a *tubulus*, as at Binchester, County Durham; (F) made of *imbrices*, curved roofing tiles; (G) shaped stone; (H) tile 'piers' similar to the floor supports in a tile kiln, at Lullingstone, Kent (diagrammatic).

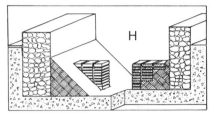

they can be seen *in situ*. Some flues were improvised, as at the bottom of the stairs at Lullingstone, where ordinary roof tiles (*tegulae*) were employed (figure 20).

No walls with flues survive to sufficient height in Britain to show us how the gases were vented to outside. Only a few examples exist elsewhere, and these may not be representative. It seems clear that where the walls were lined with flues they joined a horizontal collecting

20. Common roof tile (*tegula*). Tiles like this could be used as shallow 'hooked tiles', as at Lullingstone, Kent.

21. Mushroom-shaped clayware vent, from Pompeii.

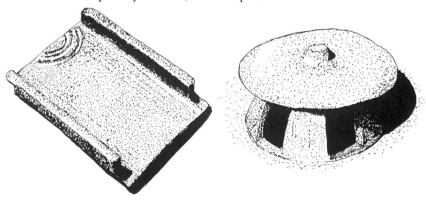

22. The baths depicted inside the Simpelveldt sarcophagus, now in Leiden museum, Holland. The *caldarium* would be on the left. There are windows with shutters and a small vent high up under the eaves.

channel at the top. In public baths at Pompeii these amounted to small tunnels which vented through pipes in the faces of walls or, in the case of the Forum Baths, vertical pipes through the flat roof, fitted with purpose-made mushroom covers (figure 21). Large 'windows' are seen in the Central Baths at Herculaneum. At the Extramural Baths at Herculaneum, the first baths completed with *tubuli*, there was a single 'factory chimney' to take the smoke clear of the town wall and the houses within, but this is a unique situation. It is, however, similar to the arrangement deduced by the excavators at Olympia (figure 2). In the vaulted Hunting Baths at Leptis Magna there were vertical chimney pipes, mainly at corners of rooms.

Some domestic baths at Pompeii have vertical chimney pipes. However, a fine example of a lean-to domestic bathing suite, attached to the House of the Silver Wedding, has openings in the vertical face of the outside wall at points corresponding to the corners of the rooms. They contain pipes which could have turned after emerging. A picture of a building carved in low relief on the inside of a Roman sarcophagus from Simpelveldt, now in Leiden museum, has been identified as a bath-house. It has a narrow slot under the eaves which could be a vent.

This detail would have prevented problems which would have been encountered in taking the chimney through a roof tiled with *tegulae* and *imbrices* (figure 22).

Ceilings and roofs

It was usual for the bathrooms to have vaulted ceilings. With large buildings lightweight materials were used to construct the vaults. These include hollow voussoirs like trapezoid *tubuli*, voussoirs of calcareous tufa, and hollow ribs made with shaped tiles or tufa, as at Chesters. It is arguable that the gases from the flues also circulated in some of the hollow vaults, since soot has been reported inside the voussoirs (figures 23 and 24).

Since the publication of the Hunting Baths at Leptis, an unusual building with exposed vaults, it has become common for reconstructions of baths to be similar structures, even where, as at Lullingstone, numerous conventional roofing tiles, yellow and red, were found. It is unlikely that baths, especially in Britain, would have looked like Nissen huts. Aesthetic considerations would have dictated that the baths would have a conventional pitched roof. At Hadrian's Villa, Tivoli, the vaults

23. Part of the vault which covered the Great Bath at Bath, made of *tubuli*.

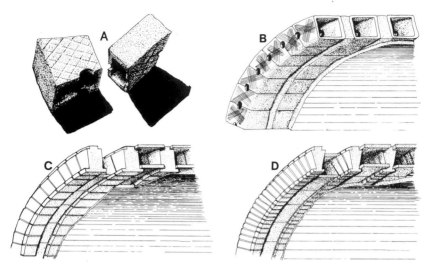

24. Lightweight vaults. (A) Hollow earthenware voussoirs. They occur on a number of sites, including Chedworth, Gloucestershire. (B) A vault constructed of these. (C) A vault using light tufa 'chair' voussoirs and two sizes of tile, as at Chesters, Northumberland. (D) Using stone or tile 'chair' voussoirs with one size of tile. Several varieties of 'chair' have been found on sites throughout Britain.

which could be seen from outside were finished in this way, with the tiles cemented in place. In any case, in Britain, because of the climate, it would have been desirable to have tiles to shed rainwater and prevent weathering.

In many of the domestic baths at Pompeii putlog holes for longitudinal beams indicate that there was a simple lightweight plaster ceiling, and other beamslots show that this was covered by a normal pitched tile roof.

From outside, baths in Britain would therefore generally appear similar to most other buildings. The windows would be glazed, but probably fitted with shutters to conserve heat — these are seen in the Simpelveldt example. There would be vents from the hypocaust, probably under the eaves.

Drains

There would have to be drains. These may have been simple ditches, as at Welwyn, properly lined gullies or even pipes.

The ever practical Romans often made use of the waste water from the baths to flush the latrines, where these were provided. They consisted of a series of perforated seats directly over an open gully.

Baths and religion

It is always easy for the archaeologist who is faced with something he does not understand to take refuge in the explanation that it is a cult object or the product of some religious activity. There does not seem to have been a specific deity of the baths, but it is well known that many of the local deities made their homes in springs, and shrines connected with springs are found throughout Britain. Coventina's Well on Hadrian's Wall is a well known example. The deity becomes particularly powerful when the waters of the spring are believed to have curative powers. The ultimate example of this is seen at Bath (*Aquae Sulis*), where the native deity, despite obvious masculine attributes, became identified with Minerva in a goddess Sulis Minerva. The Roman city owed its existence almost entirely to the temple-spa complex which developed on the site (see chapter 4).

Several military baths are known to have contained altars to or figures of Fortuna, the goddess who protected the men at their most vulnerable, when naked (figure 25).

25. Altar to Fortuna from the baths at Chesters, Northumberland.

Who used the baths?

This question can be answered on several levels. The first, the consideration of mixed bathing, has already been dealt with. With private baths it would seem likely that the whole family might use the facility together. We then have the question of whether the slaves were allowed in. Clearly personal slaves would accompany the bather; mention has already been made of Fronto being carried through the baths by his 'boys'. Slaves would also assist with undressing, dressing and wielding the strigil.

There is a story that Hadrian saw a man making use of the wall to scrape the oil from his back. The Emperor gave this poor man a slave. Next time he visited, many old men were scraping themselves on the wall, so he gave them strigils and told them to scrape one another.

Whether the ordinary household and agricultural slaves used the baths perhaps depended upon the degree of enlightenment or fastidiousness of the master. Columella says: 'It is important that there should be such places in which the servants may bathe — but only on holidays, for frequent bathing is not conducive to physical vigour.'

In many villa sites two suites of baths appear on the plan. The problem always is to know whether they were used contemporarily and, if so, what classes of people they separated. At Welwyn, for example, the baths displayed probably belonged to the steward. The others, not visible at present, were used by the master.

Military bath-houses are usually outside the forts. A number of reasons could be put forward for this. Likely ones must include that the baths were to some extent excluded from martial discipline because it is difficult to distinguish officers when they are naked. Finds of feminine objects such as jewellery and hairpins in the drains are evidence that the baths were used by the women from the *vicus*, even if mixed bathing was not allowed.

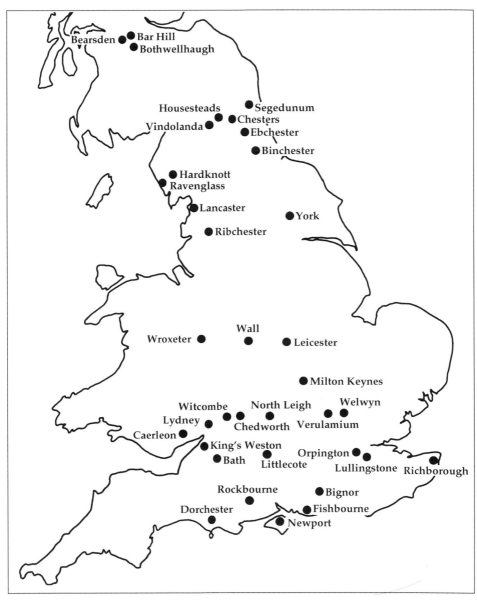

26. Location of Roman baths visible to the public and described in the gazetteer.

27. Bar Hill baths from the hot-room end. The scale is in the small *laconicum*.

28. The Great Bath at Bath. The superstructure is modern. A large piece of the original vault can be seen against the end wall.

4
Gazetteer

This brief gazetteer provides a list of all the sites in Britain which are accessible and have Roman baths displayed in some way. The author will welcome any additions or corrections to it.

No attempt has been made to classify them according to merit, largely because in many instances the site itself may be outstanding whereas the baths are poor. On other sites the baths are well worth seeing but may be indifferently displayed with no explanatory material.

For comparison the plans are all at approximately the same scale (about 1:300), with the exception of figure 72, which is at 1:400, and the isometric drawings. Small suites of baths are usually about 10 Roman feet (2.95 metres) wide, which provides a useful sense of scale. In many instances it would require considerable work, a resurvey, or perhaps even an excavation to provide better information, so only simple outlines have been provided.

The letters AM denote sites under the protection of the relevant government body. Open sites can be visited at all reasonable times.

The abbreviations used on the site plans are as follows: A, changing room (*apodyterium*); B, bath tub; C, hot (steam) room (*caldarium*); F, cold room (*frigidarium*); H, heated room, function not known; L, hot dry room (*laconicum*); N, latrine; P, stokehole (*praefurnium*); S, steam tank; ▷, north point.

Bar Hill, Strathclyde (NS 7076). AM; open site. At Twechar, approached by footpath behind war memorial. Baths inside Antonine Wall fort, of two periods. Mostly outlined in turf but some stone *pilae* are *in situ*.

Bath, Avon (ST 7564). In the centre of the city near the Abbey. Admission charge. Guidebook, museum, guided tours. One of the best known and most important sites in southern Britain. A vast spa based on a hot spring. Two large suites of heated baths which were subject to many alterations. The altar of Sulis Minerva and the front steps of her temple are exposed but underground. The visitor is recommended to follow the plan in the guidebook as the tour is somewhat labyrinthine.

29. Bar Hill. (After M. J. Moore.)

30. (Above) A view of the Bearsden baths from the cold-room end.

31. (Right) Bearsden. (After M. J. Moore.)

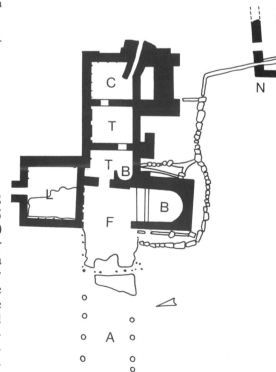

Bearsden, Strathclyde (NS 5372). AM; open site. At 35 Roman Road, on north side 150 yards (140 metres) east of car park; through a small gate in a wall. Explanatory display board. The most impressive building along the Antonine Wall, with drainage system and latrine. Stone *pilae* and jacketing. Dated to the Antonine occupation of Scotland AD 142-65.

Bignor, West Sussex (SU 9915). On a minor road from Bury to Bignor, 5 miles (8 km) south-west of Pulborough. Admission charge. An excellent guidebook and a museum on the site. Two suites of baths laid out in grass and gravel. The elaborate cold bath of one is intact. Excavation of the south baths has shown that extensive robbing took place after the original excavation.

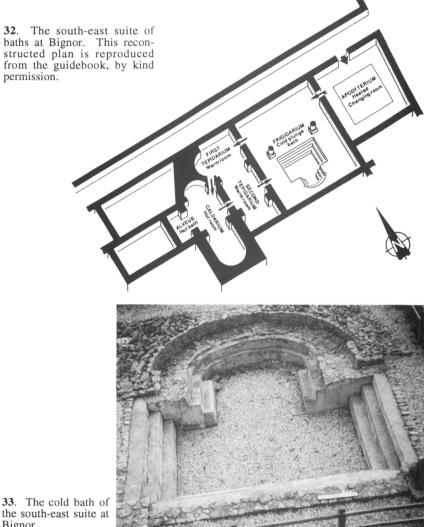

32. The south-east suite of baths at Bignor. This reconstructed plan is reproduced from the guidebook, by kind permission.

33. The cold bath of the south-east suite at Bignor.

34. Binchester. (Bowes Museum.)

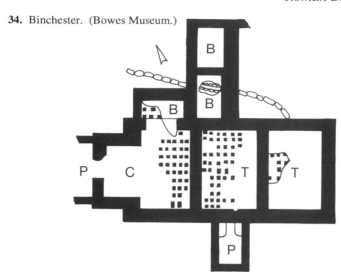

35. The Bothwellhaugh baths from the cold-room end.

Binchester, County Durham (NZ 2131). On minor road off A689. Admission charge. In a minor fort, *Vinovia*, these large baths are said to have belonged to the commandant. Under cover; probably the best preserved example of hypocausted baths in Britain, with standing *pilae* supporting a concrete floor with flues *in situ*.

Bothwellhaugh, Strathclyde (NS 7356). AM; open site. In Strathclyde Park (entrance west of M74, junction 4). Explanatory display board. The baths, which belonged to a small fort, are close to the so-called 'Roman' bridge, where they were re-erected following the flooding to form the nearby reservoir. Consolidation includes replacement of some tiles with red concrete paving slabs. Dated to the Antonine occupation of Scotland, AD 142-65.

Caerleon, Gwent (ST 3490). AM. Admission charge. The site is a legionary fortress. A part of the first-century fortress baths is displayed in a modern cover building with excellent display material. Other baths are partially uncovered on the west side of the amphitheatre, which they predate; they were altered when it was built in *c*. AD 80, to avoid obstruction of one of the entrances, but were demolished about AD 125.

36. The furnace room and part of a heated room of a suite of baths beside the amphitheatre at Caerleon.

37. The hot room, hot bath and warm room (with *pilae* and mosaic *in situ*) at Chedworth. (National Trust.)

Chedworth, Gloucestershire (SP 0513). National Trust; check opening hours before setting out. At end of minor road; signposted from A429 3 miles (5 km) north-west of Fossebridge. Admission charge. Two suites of baths in one corner of an impressive courtyard villa: the smaller well preserved with mosaic and flue tiles *in situ*; the larger complicated, multi-period, and well analysed in the guidebook. Part of an earlier, underlying suite outlined in turf.

Chesters, Northumberland (NY 9170). AM. Signposted from Chollerford on B6318. Admission charge. The extramural baths of the Hadrian's Wall fort of *Cilurnum* are among the most famous upstanding Roman buildings in Britain. They were clearly subject to considerable alteration during their long life. Exposure, robbing and early excavation make it difficult to understand the history of the site. Its remarkable preservation nevertheless makes it an excellent type site. The commandant's house has a small suite of baths as well as many heated rooms.

38. Chesters. (After Macdonald.)

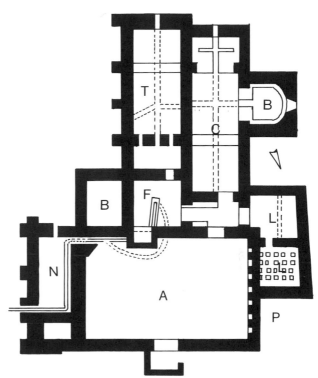

39. (Below) View from the changing-room end of Chesters fort baths.

40. The hot room of the commandant's baths at Chesters, with the furnace in the foreground.

41. These rooms in Colliton Park, Dorchester, were identified by the original excavator as a bathing suite. The stokehole of the *laconicum* is nearest the camera.

Dorchester, Dorset (SY 6990). In Colliton Park behind County Hall. The southern range of fourth-century buildings was interpreted as a suite of baths by the excavator. This is not stated in the explanatory notices.

Ebchester, County Durham (NZ 1055). In garden of Mains Farm, opposite the church, south of A689. Small private museum on site. Only the channel hypocaust of one apsidal room of an internal suite of baths of the fort of *Vindomora* is visible today.

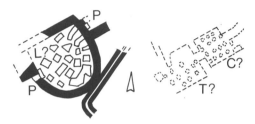

42. Ebchester. (After A. Reed.)

43. A large apsidal heated room, possibly a *laconicum*, at Ebchester.

44. (Above) The baths at Fishbourne.

45. (Below right) Fishbourne. (After Cunliffe, Society of Antiquaries.)

Fishbourne, West Sussex (SU 8405). In Salthill Road, signposted from A27 1½ miles (2.4 km) west of Chichester. Admission charge. Museum and guidebook. Part of a complex described as a palace. Small suite of baths built *c.* AD 100, demolished *c.*270. The remains are almost entirely reconstructed and set in concrete. The surviving *pilae* are not in the places shown on the plan. The stokehole is not visible.

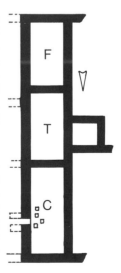

Hardknott, Cumbria (NY 2102). AM; open site. Halfway down the west side of Hardknott Pass. The extramural baths of the fort of *Mediobogdum.* Modern robbing has removed tile stokehole and hypocaust *pilae.* A fine circular *laconicum.* The fort was manned from the late first century AD to the early second, when it became a wayside resting place for travellers.

46. (Above) View over the baths at Hardknott from the cold-room end, with the circular *laconicum* at the left.

47. (Right) Hardknott.

48. (Below) King's Weston. (After G. C. Boon.)

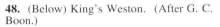
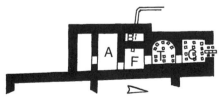

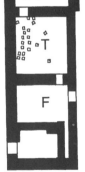

Housesteads Roman Fort, Northumberland (NY 7969). On Hadrian's Wall 2.25 miles (3 km) north-east of Bardon Mill off B6318. Two suites of baths: one in building XI next to the commandant's house (*praetorium*); the other built into barrack block XV next to the main gate.

King's Weston, Bristol (ST 5377). About 2 miles (3 km) north of Sea Mills. Keys obtainable from Blaise Castle Museum, along with instructions for finding the site. The baths are part of a preserved late third-century villa. The mosaics were brought here from elsewhere.

49. The baths at Lancaster, partially cut through by a later V-shaped ditch.

Lancaster, Lancashire (SD 4961). Reached from a signposted footpath below the Priory: it is about 100 metres off the path, near the modern buildings, under the Wery Wall. Viewed through railings. Partially cut through by the ditch of the fourth-century fort.

Leicester, Leicestershire (SK 5804). Off St Nicholas Circle in city centre. Display plan and museum. Most of the (outlined) foundations of large second-century town baths. The Jewry Wall is part of the party wall with the basilica, comparable with the 'Old Work' at Wroxeter.

Littlecote, Wiltshire (SU 3070). In Littlecote Park 2 miles (3.2 km) north-west of Hungerford. There are three suites of baths: one in the north building (Building 1), next to the Orphic rooms; one at the south end of the west building (Building 3) and one built into the north side of the south building (Building 6). An apse near the south-west corner of Building 6 is part of an unfinished suite of baths.

Lullingstone, Kent (TQ 5365). AM. 1 mile (1.6 km) west of Eynsford at end of minor road off A225. Admission charge. Display of finds, recorded commentary, explanatory display boards. The site, under cover, of an extraordinary villa. Late second-century baths with an unusual plan. The long narrow *caldarium* has piers rather than *pilae* (figure 19). Alterations in the fourth century include raising of floor levels.

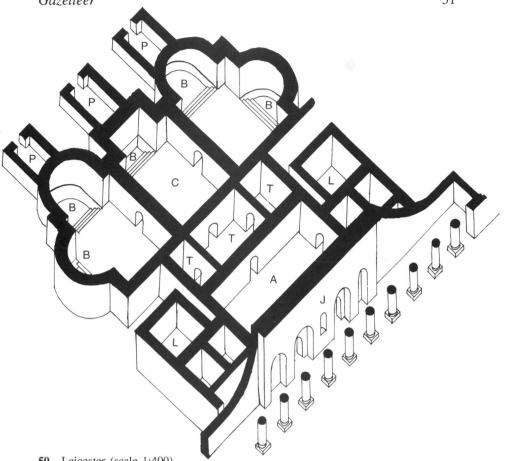

50. Leicester (scale 1:400).
J indicates the Jewry Wall.

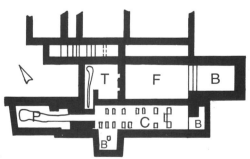

51. Lullingstone.

Lydney, Gloucestershire (SO 6203). Private; can be visited by written permission of the Estate Office, Lydney. The baths are part of a temple complex erected very late in the fourth century; part of a healing sanctuary.

Milton Keynes, Buckinghamshire (SP 3983). Bancroft Roman Villa, in open land south of Miller's Way. The reconstructed foundations of a villa contain baths.

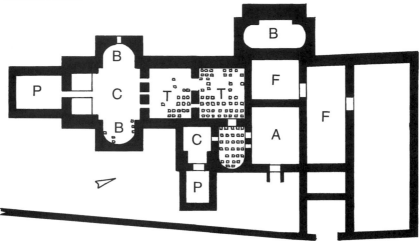

52. Lydney. (After R. E. M. Wheeler, Society of Antiquaries.)

53. The principal heated rooms of the Lydney baths from the north-east, with the main furnace in the background.

Newport, Isle of Wight (SZ 5088). Avondale Road. Admission charge. Displays, small guidebook. A fine suite of baths, part of a late second-century winged-corridor villa, with mosaics, flue tiles *in situ*. Excellent preservation.

North Leigh, Oxfordshire (SP 3915). AM. Off A4095 3 miles (5 km) north-east of Witney. Admission charge. One suite of baths of a large courtyard villa, with earlier ones outlined in gravel beneath, close to custodian's building.

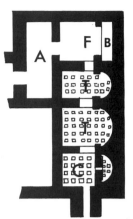

54. (Above) Newport. (After P. G. Stone, Society of Antiquaries.)

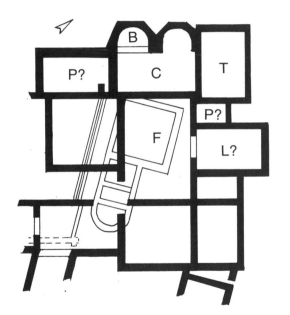

55. (Left) North Leigh. (After N. V. Taylor.)

56. (Below) Orpington. (After S. Palmer, London Borough of Bromley.)

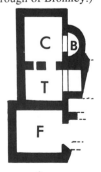

Orpington, Greater London (TQ 4768). For admission apply to the Curator, London Borough of Bromley Museum, The Priory, Church Hill, Orpington BR6 0HH. Enclosed and covered remains of a small, probably third-century suite of baths.

57. View of the visible remains of the Ravenglass baths from the south-west. The cold room is nearest the camera.

Ravenglass, Cumbria (SD 0896). AM; open site. Reached by a drive from village. Spectacularly upstanding walls of part of the extramural baths of the fort of *Glannaventa*, with window splays, internal rendering and a wall niche. The fort was built in the late first century and occupied into the fifth century.

58. Ribchester. (After K. Ford.)

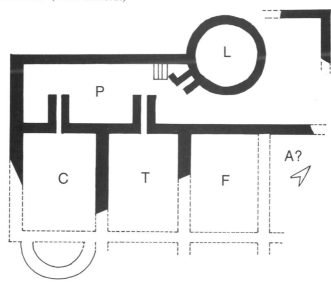

59. The circular *laconicum* at Ribchester.

Ribchester, Lancashire (SD 6535). Limited opening. Village on B6245 north of Blackburn. Baths behind the White Bull, also signposted from the museum. Second-century baths of the Roman fort.

Richborough, Kent (TR 3260). AM. 1½ miles (2.4 km) north of Sandwich on minor road off A257. Admission charge. Baths of Saxon Shore fort sitting on the earlier remains of the *mansio* (posting station).

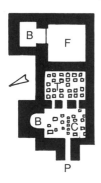

60. (Above) Richborough. (After Bushe-Fox, Society of Antiquaries.)

61. (Right) The small suite of baths over the *mansio* at Richborough from the hot-room end.

62. The east bath suite at Rockbourne. The heated rooms and hot bath are outlined in turf.

Rockbourne, Hampshire (SU 1217). 2 miles (3 km) west of Fording-bridge, off A354 or B3078. Admission charge. Small museum, display boards. Most of the excavations have been backfilled for protection. The main features are the hypocausts and mosaics. Most of the walls are shown as bands of gravel, and the major post holes by truncated posts. There are two suites of baths. The north-west baths have *pilae* made from *imbrices*. The others have elaborate mosaics and cold bath.

Segedunum (Wallsend), Northumberland (NZ 3066). Buddle Street, south of A187. Tourist signposts. A modern working full-sized suite of

63. The west bath suite at Rockbourne. Note the *pilae* of *imbrices* in the hot room.

64. At Segedunum (Wallsend) this modern reconstruction of the bath-house at Chesters has been built and is open to the public. (Photograph: Cadbury Lamb.)

baths based on a mirror-image of the remains of the baths at Chesters affords the visitor the valuable experience of something like the authentic environment.

Verulamium, Hertfordshire (TL 1307). Limited hours. The mosaic with composite hypocaust on display in a bungalow in the park west of St Albans was identified by the excavator as the *tepidarium* of a bathing suite belonging to a second-century town house.

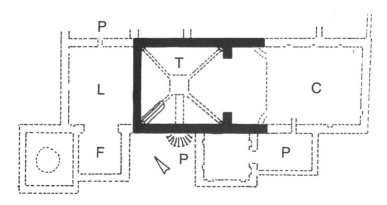

65. Verulamium. (After R. E. M. Wheeler, Society of Antiquaries.)

66. Verulamium. This photograph of the mosaic with composite hypocaust was taken at the time of the excavation by Tessa and Mortimer Wheeler in the early 1930s. (Courtesy of the St Albans Museum Service.)

67. The Wall baths from the stokehole end. The scale stands where the *pilae* have been reburied.

Vindolanda (Chesterholme), Northumberland (NY 7764). Signposted from the B8316 ¹/₂ mile west of Housesteads car park. Admission charge. Two military bath houses are on view: the late-first-century one outside the Stone Fort on the south, and the early-third-century one, north-west of the Stone Fort. There are also two bath suites in commanding officers' residences.

Wall, Staffordshire (SK 0906). AM. Just off the A5 near Brownhills. Admission charge. Elaborate baths were part of a *mansio*. Easily appreciated at a superficial level, the site is confusing because several periods are visible. The hypocaust has been filled in and turfed over but can be seen in photographs on display and in the guidebook.

Welwyn, Hertfordshire (TL 2315). Entrance from middle roundabout on Welwyn bypass. Admission charge. One suite of baths of a third-century villa complex preserved in a steel vault under the embankment of the A1(M).

68. Welwyn.

69. Welwyn Roman baths from the cold-room end. The wall through the centre of the picture is the end wall of the villa, with the cold and hot baths projecting. Outside these are excavators' trenches.

Witcombe, Gloucestershire (SO 8914). AM; open site, but key needed to view the best preserved baths (the key is obtainable from Corinium Museum, Cirencester.) Accessible by a long drive south of the A417, just east of the junction with the A46. A preserved villa in beautiful surroundings. Two suites of baths. One multi-period and complicated suite is partially covered by small modern buildings and includes a naive mosaic of sea creatures. The best preserved hypocaust is hidden under a low flat felt roof.

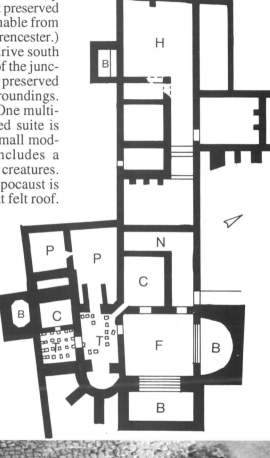

70. (Right) Witcombe. (After E. Greenfield, English Heritage.)

71. (Below) The fish mosaic in the cold room at Witcombe.

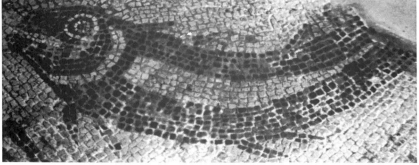

Wroxeter, Shropshire (SJ 5608). AM. By B4380 or B4394 south of A5. Admission charge. Excellent display boards of plans and reconstructions. Museum. The huge second-century baths include one of the largest pieces of upstanding Roman masonry in Britain — the 'Old Work' — bounding the basilica, and comparable with the Jewry Wall at Leicester (see figure 50).

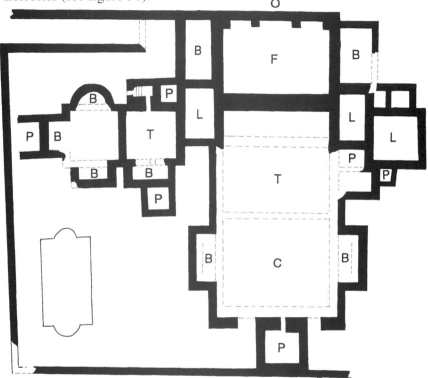

72. Wroxeter (scale 1:400). O indicates the Old Work.

York, North Yorkshire (SE 6052). In the cellars of the Roman Bath Inn, Church Street; visible through a glass panel in the saloon bar. Open during licensing hours. The *caldarium* with *pilae* bases and part of the tiled *frigidarium* of fourth-century baths.

73. York. (After P. Corder.)

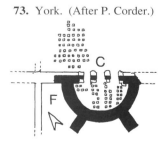

5
Further reading

The historical argument of this Shire Archaeology book was published by the author in *Roman Brick and Tile* (BAR International Series 68, 1979), pages 303-8, and the *Journal of Archaeological Science*, 5 (1978), pages 269-82. The latter paper contains a detailed bibliography of ancient and modern sources and indicates how the fuel consumption of a suite of baths — the ones at Welwyn — could be calculated.

The first work in the English language specifically on the subject of Roman baths, *Thermae et Balnea* by Inge Nielsen, was published by Aarhus University Press in two volumes in 1990. It deals almost exclusively with the architecture and cultural history of public baths throughout the Empire and contains a very extensive bibliography.

For individual sites, guidebooks and original excavation reports are most useful — where they exist. Two outstanding general guides are *Roman Remains in Britain*, by Roger J. A. Wilson (Constable, 1988), and *Scotland's Roman Remains*, by Lawrence Keppie. They assist both with locating sites and with finding out where site reports were published, usually in academic or local society publications which are available only in large or special libraries.

Almost every general work on Roman Britain contains some information on baths. For a classicist's view of the social and cultural importance of baths to metropolitan Romans Jerome Carcopino's *Daily Life in Ancient Rome* (Penguin, 1991) is worth reading; it and Vitruvius's *Ten Books on Architecture*, translated by Morris Hickey Morgan (Dover, 1960), are available in paperback.

Roman building materials are discussed in *A History of Building Materials* by Norman Davey (Phoenix House, 1961), *Roman Brick and Tile* by Gerald Brodribb (Alan Sutton, 1987) and in Shire Archaeology number 24, *Roman Crafts and Industries* by Alan McWhirr (Shire, 1982; reprinted 1988).

Index

Page numbers in italic refer to illustrations.